The Dialogue of a HEART and MIND Disconnect

*It is unusual that one finds a title first,
but as thoughts flow outward, feelings are condensed.
Now it is time to make sense of events past, present, and future.*

Pamela Schuyler

ISBN 978-1-953223-58-6 (paperback)

Copyright © 2020 by Pamela Schuyler

All rights reserved. No part of this publication may be reproduced, distributed, or transmitted in any form or by any means, including photocopying, recording, or other electronic or mechanical methods without the prior written permission of the publisher. For permission requests, solicit the publisher via the address below.

Rushmore Press LLC
1 800 460 9188
www.rushmorepress.com

Printed in the United States of America

Contents

Introduction v

The Story 1
Trying to Understand…Not Understanding 9
Psychiatrist's Notes and My Comments 15
Letters to My Husband 27
A Series of Thoughts Written Down 33
Text and Phone Communications 75
Trying To Understand This Illness 116
Eastern and Western Medical Explanations
for Clinical Depression 128
Improving Communication 137
The Questions for the Living 146
Facts, Not Fiction 148
And This Is Not the End 153

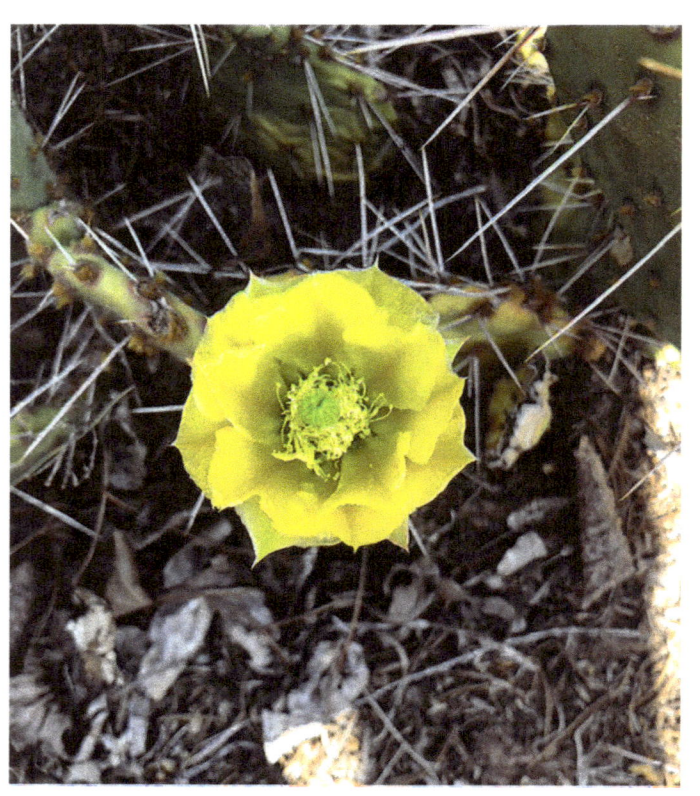

Introduction

The Dialogue of a Heart and Mind Disconnect took many years to come into being. Throughout the years, I wrote down many thoughts since I had no one to share my feelings with about my crumbling relationship with my husband. I finally realized I was part of a repetitive story and wanted to change it.

I realized that others might also get some use from these offerings.
We are not alone in our sufferings.
We need support.

We watch tides rise up on both sides of us. Here in the middle, with hope, perseverance, and determination, we fight to survive until the end. Here we can accept loss and move on or perish mentally, physically, emotionally, and spiritually.

With compassion to so many who suffer.

The Story

I grew up in a middle-class family. My mother was always right, with no room for discussion. I think this was a cover for insecurity and possibly the beginning of her depression. My father was always working and on the road. As it turned out, he also had lady friends on his journeys. After my mother's discovery, years later, she became very angry and developed clinical depression.

This was the household I grew up in. I was always trying to make things better for both my parents but never succeeded. After all, I was only a child.

School became important to me, partially as an escape from family. In third grade, I had three amazing teachers who inspired me to become a teacher after I had something to teach. *(Yoga and art history became my two gigs.)*

In middle school, there was another great teacher who inspired me to write.

In high school, I felt more stifled. Much memorization was needed, and I really had to study to understand and retain information.

I was determined to succeed in my studies at college. I discovered art history and photography, which became my passions. Photography became my profession, art history became my foundation.

As a woman was trained in those days, love was far more important than a career, so I got married and moved to be with the man I loved. Because I was in love, my husband's career came first. I accepted this at some level. I worked in photography part-time. After my husband completed his residency, he became a physician. He listened carefully to patients; hearing things other people had missed. His secondary passion was economics, which got him more involved with economics in medicine. Losing contact with individual people moved him closer to his clinical depression. Long gray winters in the town he worked in was another push toward an illness that went undiagnosed. We all assumed he was just a quiet, introverted, and shy academic since childhood. These too were indications for possibilities of depression that no one paid attention to.

He was very studious. He advanced in school quickly and went to college at the age of sixteen. He always told me how frustrated he was because he could not matriculate easily in college. He was too young to enjoy dating and socializing, so he became more introverted and studied even more. Another push.

These are the brief histories of the two characters that create "*The Dialogue of a Heart and Mind Disconnect*"

In our early years, we enjoyed each other's company, and we would talk forever. We became very good friends. We were very close. We got married.

We found a house close to work. I continued to work in photography. My husband advanced in his medical profession. As I recall, he was always frustrated and never satisfied with how he was treated by his superiors. He felt he was never appreciated enough, which hurt him deeply, another clue unnoticed to underlying depression. He kept switching jobs, moving us frequently to find his praise. He ignored and undervalued the support of his wife and family. He was very successful at work yet never felt he was good enough. Over time, his perception of lack of appreciation weakened his spirit and heart. He was seeking the impossible. He took another job in another cold and rainy city. It was a terrible climate for an introvert and someone who suffered from depression, now diagnosed. I never realized he suffered from depression because he was so lively at work.

His mind took him a long way before it stifled his heart. Again, his illness was ignored. At one point, we moved to a sunny, warm city, which did help lighten his spirits for a while. He actually got into yoga and meditation. His job in the sun was tough because he had to cut unproductive programs for the company. People did not like him for that. Another push toward illness.

Over time, I realized that though he said he worked for both of us, I came in second. This was very difficult for me to accept. It felt like I was in last place and there was nothing I could do about it. There was always distance, space, and time between us. There was only time for work and very little time for me and for us. His work became an addiction. It probably always was. He was in his own world. He was a man who wanted to become very important in his field. He did succeed at a price—at a very high price that eventually took his life. He separated himself from his wife and family. He worked so long and hard that he lost contact with good health and his wife's strong support.

One day, he ignored the flu. He had to work. He got so sick he was hospitalized. He waited too long to see a doctor. Flu affected his heart *(a weak spot for those who suffer from depression)*. He developed atrial fibrillation. He went back to work.

We moved many times for his career. My photography was no longer viable in terms of a career for myself. I got more involved in fine art. I was no slouch when it came to art and cooking.

Art and cooking kept me creative and busy while my husband, addicted to work, continued to have very little time for us together. He stopped exercising and socializing outside of work. He had no time. He only had time for work. I became an inconvenience.

In my art field, I used yoga to help me center and focus. Through yoga, a practice of medicine from India came to my attention called Ayurveda, which helps balance imbalances. The medical practice of Ayurveda has existed in India for several thousand years. It answered questions that I could not get answers for from Western medicine. To be healthy through Ayurveda seemed logical. Health was encouraged through diet, lifestyle, exercise, massage, and herbs. Ayurveda was a preventative and supportive approach to well-being mentally, physically, and spiritually. I was hungry to learn more, eventually receiving my second MA in Ayurveda. *(My first master's degree was an MFA in photography.)* I developed a client base in Ayurveda and yoga, my new art practice. It was time to give back. My clients became my artwork that I could send home to their families, usually feeling better.

This was a wonderful substitute for not having children, which my husband never wanted.

My husband continued to slip more into himself and work. His obsession with work kept him away from home longer and longer, until he was diagnosed with full-blown clinical depression. When he came home, he was silent, gobbled a good meal down, watched TV, and went into the back room to sleep alone. This went on for many years. I was unable to help. He didn't like my telling him truth about his work addiction or depression. He tuned me out. Why would a physician want to listen to his wife?

Unable to offer help, I became frustrated, which moved to anger. I was an outsider. After all the years of proofing his papers and preparing meals for his colleagues, I was no longer part of the family I wanted to be part of. He could not hear information from me or his psychologist and psychiatrist. He manipulated the system in his ill health behavior. He was bright and he was arrogant. He kept all of us at a distance. He had to work. He had little interest in making friends, with no hobbies outside of work. He only traveled for work.

My husband had no adventures unless I dragged
him along. He would write in notebooks, in
very small handwriting about trivia he could
impress his colleagues with. All therapeutic
information he received from his doctors
was applied at work, never at home.
With my new studies in Ayurveda, I was able
to encourage him to practice some breathing
techniques, some meditation, some yoga,
and some study in Sanskrit. He also applied
these positives to work, not family. He briefly
participated in life outside of work because of
Ayurveda. Eventually, he described this and me
as too much trouble. He went back to work. His
fatigue increased, leading to more bad health.

This distancing moved me to take notes,
write prose, write poetry, write letters,
take photographs, write down thoughts,
research depression, and find statistics.

I hope some of my observations may allow
us to recognize earlier signs of clinical
depression and to hear silent cries for help.

I share with you *"The Dialogue of a
Heart and Mind Disconnect"*

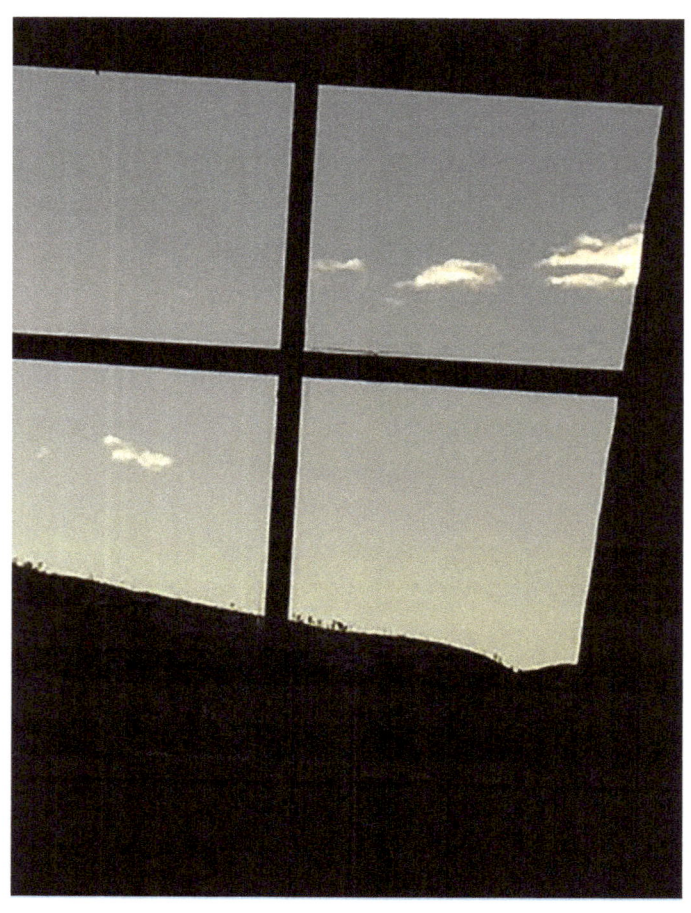

Trying to Understand...
Not Understanding

There has been a distancing for
many tears/years now.
I felt hurt when connection could not be made.
Without connection, I took things personally.

It took many years to understand what was
wrong. It took many years to think I could make
things better for us, which I could not make better.
I tried to take things into my own hands, even
though the events were outside myself.
He is the sufferer, and I suffered.

I was an outsider because of the
relationship that had disappeared into
dislocation, disregard, and isolation.
I moved with him from one job to another.
I changed my personality.
I thought about what I had done wrong.
He said it was only himself.
How could that be?

I tried to figure out what was going on.
We stepped further back from ourselves.
We sought therapy, yet only
the healthy one heard.

Again, more on my shoulders.
What did this mean?
How could I fix this?

If I could only work harder.
If I could find another way to fix the relationship.
I became more independent.
I could not fix him; I could only take care of myself.
I became more creative. I studied
depression through thoughts, books, papers,
physicians, therapists, and articles.
I was in the same story.

He did not change.
He buried himself in work so deeply. He described
himself as getting out of a dark hole every
morning until he could no longer get out.

My independence continued.
I put more creativity into my work.
I figured out my mother also suffered from
depression, which is why my mother and
my husband communicated so well.

I developed friendships with upbeat humans.
My mate slipped further down the rabbit
hole through his addiction to work, his ego,
and his looking down upon others.

I thought this must be okay.
I mistook brilliance for arrogance.
More distance.
Many years passed.
I came second to his work, and I
now understand this is reality.

The reality was my husband was
addicted to work, not working for us.

This reality existed for many years of marriage.
He had always denied this.
He said his work was for both of us.

Both of us recognized his work addiction, though
he ignored it and I accepted this behavior.
My frustration and anger increased, and he
blamed my anger for his withdrawal from the
relationship. *(My anger came from my frustration
from being in second place, his unawareness of
his clinical depression and his addiction to work.)*
He began to work in a different state.

He no longer came home.
I no longer wanted him to disrupt my life
because he only came home to sleep,
stare into space and be silent.
His depression made him jump into a dark hole,
consuming his once-clear mind and big heart.

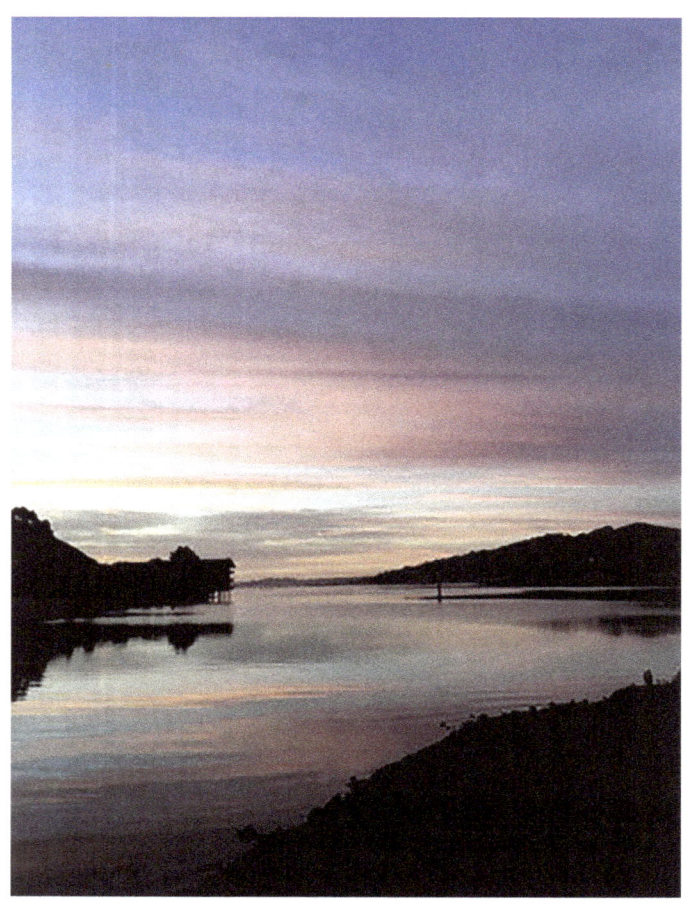

Lungs connect with grief.
Liver absorbs anger.
Kidneys hold fear.
Hear- is affected by hurt and sorrow.

These relationships find the weakest
point in the body to destroy.[1]

---

[1] Studies with Dr. Vasant Lad, Ayurvecic Institute, Albuquerque, New Mexico.

Psychiatrist's Notes and My Comments

Psychiatrist 1,
1992
"He will never change."

I am a strong woman.
I can help.
I can proof his papers to be published.
I can make fine meals.
I can set up a household anywhere he moves us.
I can create a home for him from
one coast to another.
I grow older.
This weight of two people gets heavier.

Psychiatrist 2

June 21, 2000

Nearest Relative:
Wife

Appearance and General Behavior:
His dress is neat.
His posture is tense.
His facial expression is sad.
His physical activity is underactive.

Emotional Reaction:
His attitude is reserved, scared, and sad.

His Talk:
The form is logical.
The rate is undertalkative. The quality is controlled.

His Expressions:
He has suicidal thoughts.

Does the Patient Know Who He Is?
Yes.

Does the Patient Know Where He Is?
Yes.

Date?
Yes.

How He Feels?
Yes.

General Knowledge: President?
Yes.
Pursuant to the provisions of the law as amended, the respondent was taken into custody by the undersigned and detained for a seventy-two-hour treatment and evaluation at hospital.

Conclusion:
The respondent appears to be mentally ill, and as a result of such mental illness, he appears to be in imminent danger to himself.

Psychiatrist's Notes:
Patient referred to hospital emergency room by psychiatrist. "Patient has suicidal ideation with plan to drive off mountain road. Has stopped car to look at appropriate ravines. Plans to cut self with knife. Has taken knives out to look at them and held knife to wrist."

Husband and Wife Discussion:
He told me he did this to get attention.
I told him his suicide would cause pain to
himself, me, and his family and friends.
He listened without hearing.
He was numb.
I sought help from family, who thought it must
be my fault. After all, he was a brilliant fellow.
Where was my support?

Treatment:
-Prozac
-Talk therapy
-Darkness revisited www.depressioncentral.com
(For a man who does not like working
with computers, he searches.)
He went back to work.

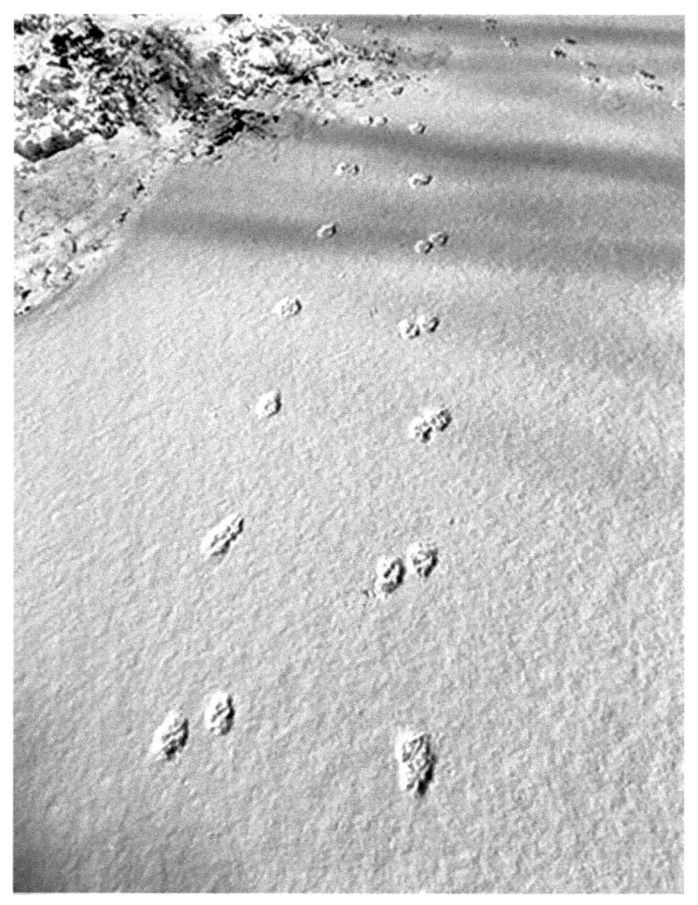

This was my first introduction to clinical depression when my husband made his first attempt at suicide. This was approximately ten years before his successful suicide death.

This suicide attempt was bizarre. It happened when he was not around me, and I received a call from a hospital where he turned himself in. I was alone. This news put me in shock. I was driving when I received this news via cell phone. I was unable to get other information because the only person who could release the information to me was my husband, who was obviously in no condition to release information.

I walked into the hospital, where I had to be screened via a metal detector to see if I carried potential weapons—weapons like long socks, belts, nail clippers, a nail file, a penknife. These items didn't occur to me to be weapons. I saw before me what was once an animated husband who was now in the throes of Prozac numbness and fog. My shock continued. I was not prepared, and I had no one other than my husband to talk to—no one to discuss him with or share the shock. He had moved us again, so I had no close people to share with. I never thought of signing up with a therapist before, never thought I needed one.

I was okay.

Finally, there was some coherency, and this man, my husband, who I thought I knew and loved, could talk. He said, "I did this to get attention." What was this? A cry for help? He cut his wrist with a paring knife. This was why the suicide attempt was not successful, he was looking for help. He did not want to kill himself.

Finally, after days of him being dazed, I received permission to meet with his psychiatrist. I could sit in on a meeting. I watched a discussion between the psychiatrist and my husband. I listened baffled, shocked, confused. I thought this must be a dream, better described as a nightmare. I thought this man was strong and brilliant. I didn't have a clue that suicide was a possibility.

He came home, still under the influence of drugs. He lost his ability to feel and work through issues he had with himself or me. He was numb. The medicine helped block emotions, so he could exist and go back to work, not allowing the patient to discover what moved him to this state.

I had an idea I thought might help. Unfortunately, this came from a point of my not understanding the disease, the medication, or the clinical depression. I was not part of this because I did not have this illness. I was healthy.

I spoke to him from my perspective. I confirmed he was asking for help. I asked which knife he took from the knife set. Again, I never thought of these as weapons, just tools for chopping, cutting, and slicing food for a wonderful recipe. The brand-new, expensive set we had invested in were not weapons for destruction. He showed me he used the paring knife.

I told him to take this knife and break the blade in the driveway and bury it. I thought this could represent burying the incident and the pain. I talked to him about how much pain he had caused me and his parents, how much sadness this had caused me, and how much his death would have created great tragedy in the family. I thought he heard. Again, this illness did not allow for social consciousness and understanding. He was unavailable. He could not understand the feelings of someone outside himself. He could not see how this violent action to himself could affect his wife and other people who cared about him. This verbiage did not register. There was no connection.

This was the sick mind, the illness. Depression is so self-involving that the person suffering from it cannot understand that this violent act not only affects himself but others. Committing suicide affects all of his friends, his relatives, and his colleagues. It sends shudders through the entire community. The illness numbs him to this awareness of affecting others. The medicines he was prescribed numbed him for months. He had no interest in talking further. He had no interest in any physical relationship—no holding hands, no hugs. He was no longer present outside of work, where he gave the greatest performances of his life. He had a glimmer of awareness about health when I began my studies in Ayurveda, and he attempted yoga and meditation for several years, which did make him more social at home.

Again, clinical depression took over.

My observations of his clinical depression:

- Stage 1: His studious childhood—isolation.
- Stage 2: College and early career—continued isolation.
- Stage 3: His inability to combine work with marriage until his first suicide attempt—inability to understand emotions.
- Stage 4: Control with exercise and diet and intervals of medicine.
- Stage 5: Overwhelming issues from the disease stops him from remaining healthy.
- Stage 6: Achieves his end game of death via successful suicide.

(After his first attempt at suicide, I waited days, months, and years for that other shoe to drop. One cannot help but wait for the next event, hoping it will never happen. Somewhere in your heart and mind and soul, filed deep down inside, you still wait.)

Letters to My Husband

May 16, 2000

Dear husband

I want to be with you so badly, and yet because you won't really address the issues I need addressed, I can't be close to you. You must really get some help so you actually understand what I am talking about, because I don't see any resolution until then. Speaking to a good therapist will make you understand how to respond to what I need, and to what you need. This isn't just a selfish matter. It will make your spirit rise. It will open your heart to help you in everything you do. You will find peace, strength, time to do things you want and inner strength to take on the sorrows of the day. I see you as a nut (seed) locked in a shell. You have closed yourself off within your own walls and stopped sharing love and joy. May you find the soil to nourish yourself and make you open up and grow into a warm, healthy sapling.

Love, Wife

Dearest husband,

You have presented me with a most difficult task that becomes necessary for me to do. This note comes from the bottom of my heart with more love for you than you may never know. It is time for you to step up to the plate and take that scientific step, that leap of faith. If you really love me, love your work, love your family, love you, it is your time to show it.
You must understand with all of your mind and heart *what you must do*.
Do not delegate. Do not ignore. Do not pass off. You must show your stuff by understanding others and rising to their needs. It is a large task that you may not know how to do yet. Your safety nets are gone. It is up to you alone to succeed in what you want to succeed in. You can become great because of who you are and what you are capable of becoming.
Along with fear, take positive steps now in understanding others (for them, not for your advantage) and fearlessly answer questions about why you really do the things you do.

If you really want to get better, it is you who must take this on all by yourself, using the tools others have generously given you for so many years. You must know the success as a physician you are in *your capable hands* to succeed or fail. The knowledge you have received over the years will guide you to success if you use this knowledge wisely. Our relationship's success is in your *capable hands and heart* if you allow all that has been given you to enlighten you and give back with true love, selfless love.
Your life is in *your capable hands* if you choose to live it with kindness, gentleness, caring, and loving yourself and others.
Your lifestyle is in *your capable hands*.
Choose where you really want to live.
Do it. Now is the time to act.
I have nothing further to add until you know what you want to do and how you want to live and smile with others. I am off.
Much love, my darling husband.
I pray for your success.

Wife

A Series of Thoughts Written Down

Old age is watching the sparkle
disappear from your lover's eyes.
When touch is an effort and
tenderness disappears.
Events that change and no longer take care of.
Ahh, touch.
The magic that withered as winter years
teach us to live with loneliness.

Misunderstood

Brilliance for arrogance.
Strength for addiction.

Spaces so wide we can breathe.

We can hear the air under the wings of ravens.
Earth shows us art forms we
could never believe true,
and man makes his mark.

(Written in 1999)

Away, far away,
yet communication is always near.
How strange we are.
Where do our comforts lie?

Suffering

Arrogance versus brilliance.
Power versus truth.
Drugs versus enlightenment.
Me versus we.
I versus divine.
Aged fear versus fearless youth.
Silence versus thanks.

Fighting for immortality is our human bondage.

Not being heard causes illness.
Being alone versus independent makes us fragile.

Everyone has different strengths and weaknesses.
With a little patience, there is kindness.

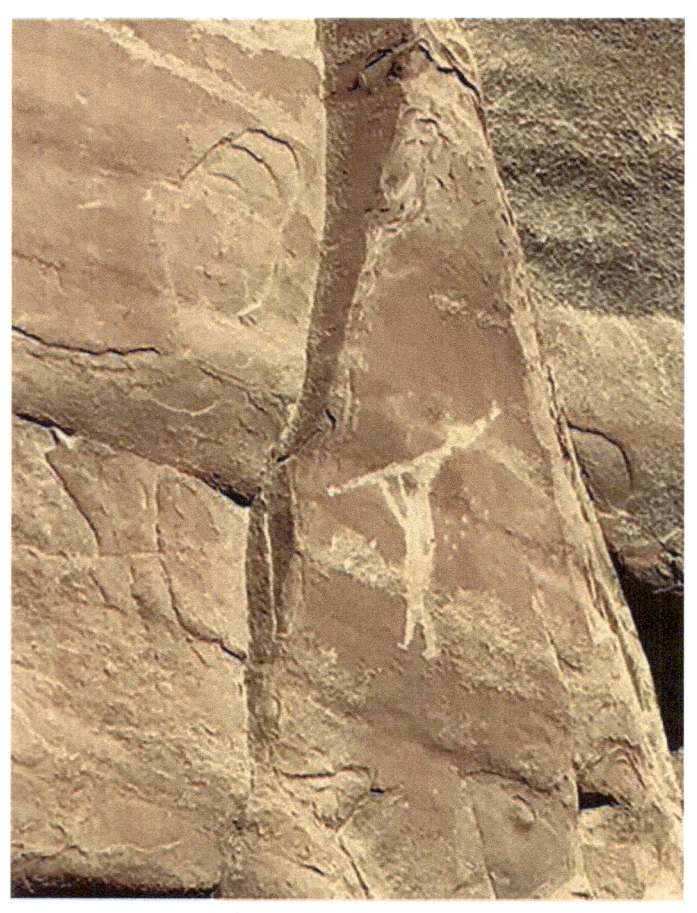

*(In the land of innocence, before I actually had a
head-on collision with depression, I truly believed
we all had the capability to be happy. These
tools are not available to those who suffer.)*

No matter who we are or where
we are or what we are
or why we are,
we have skills to be happy or not.
We have received a gift, roots of
strength for well-being.

And so this outsider continues to peel back
the skin of the sour cherries of pain.

His Letter

*(This was a handwritten letter on yellow lined
sheets of paper with minimal punctuation.
I discovered it in his accounting book
where he kept records for taxes. I found
this note when he was out of town.
This attempt was not realized.)*

Dearest wife,

My entire life has been spent cultivating an image of intellectual brilliance that has been fed by my own interior drive that has focused all of my energies on this image and by my ability to suck energy from those around me. This single focus has led me to shortchange those around me, especially you.

I can no longer sustain this effort and my
arrogance in focusing my life on this image.
It has finally become so clear that I cannot
ignore it. I have come to my end as I have lived
alone, isolated in my mind. You are the person
who has been closest to me and has sustained
me, but I have not supported you. It has been a
one-way street. I cannot ask you to forgive me
for my actions, since they are not forgivable.
I can only thank you for the thirty-six years of
comfort and support that you have given me
and for always standing by me, even when you
were in great pain because of my actions.
I only wish I understood my hated
arrogance sooner before it destroyed
me and your happiness.
I have driven to the overlook to
be joined with the ocean.

Husband

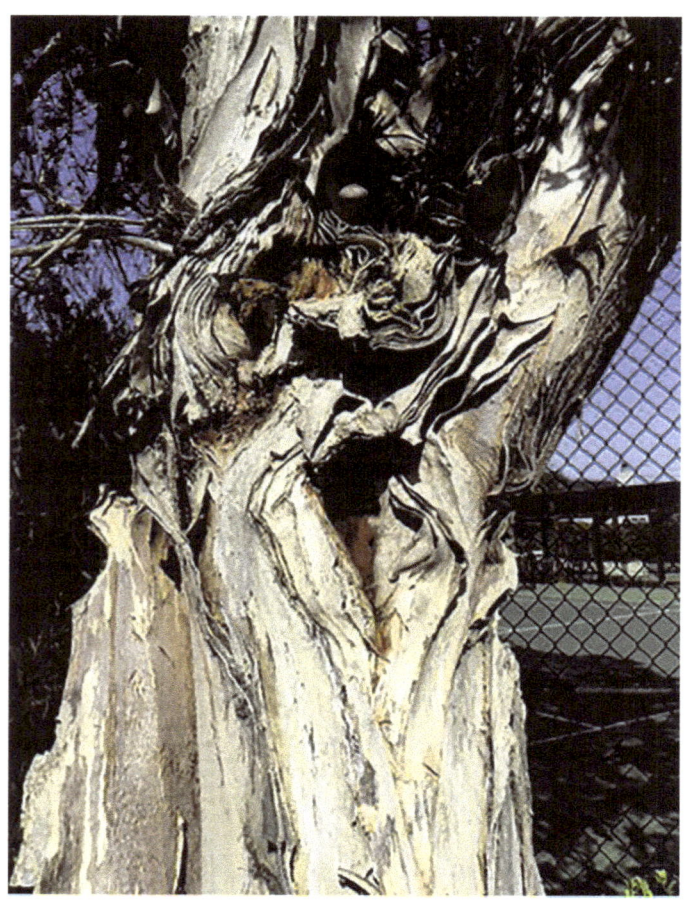

Living in the moment allows us to evolve.

Earth,

Water,

Fire,

Air,

Space

are what we are made of.
The balancing is ours to work with.

Our safety net is knowing we are not alone.
We are enveloped in everything.
We are part of everything.
We take comfort in this knowledge.

Compassion emerges from wisdom.
Understanding flourishes.

I always felt as if I was on the periphery, watching.
I was not aware of my value.
I became an observer who stopped observing myself.

As dewdrops turn to tears of changing seasons,
winter captures them and turns
tears into diamonds.

There is a fine line between
greatness and madness.
Perhaps the difference between the two
is the ability to take on responsibility.

Her heart cries out for herself.
She had accepted it is acceptable
not to be heard.
It was okay to be ignored.
The good child told the bad child,
beaten then forgiven.
This parent training allows unacceptable
actions to happen and be forgiven.

She feels fragile. She has to let go
of taking care of each other.
She realizes she has to take care of herself.
She learns protection is when something
doesn't feel good, she shouldn't do it.
If something is too difficult, she is
tired and doesn't want to fight.
She must give herself permission to let things go.

My life progressed.
I tried to be a chameleon to fit in.
I tried to reinvent myself to be with someone.
This time I reinvented myself again,
but this time it was for me.
It is difficult to get over memories.
I must leave some behind.
This time tears and laughter are mine.
I am who I am, like it or leave it,
with love and compassion for myself.

When he is depressed,
she finds it very difficult to understand.
She takes his actions personally.

The relationship gets confused with lack of
understanding of this debilitating illness
and the suffering he is going through.

The combination of the depression and work
addiction increases effects of the illness.

Text and Phone Communications

November 11, 2013
A phone message left on my cell phone.

Husband
Wife, right now I feel completely dead inside from
the depression, both about the money and just
how I feel and how afraid I am for the future.
I know—I agree with you.
I am not treating you well.
I am not disputing that.
But right now I am struggling to survive,
and I am giving it all I've got.
You are a great person, not a
bad person, obviously.
Obviously, you never have done
anything to deserve this,
and it's grossly unfair that it has happened to you,
but I am trying to figure out
what I can do about it.
I am sorry I did not come straight to you,
that I thought I was going to meet you
and didn't talk to you about it first
before I launched myself off.
I am sorry I am in such bad shape,
and I am sorry you got stuck with me.
I am sorry I cannot deliver what you need at
an emotional level and a physical level,
and you have every right to be mad and upset.

October 2013 until August 2014

Text messages.

The dialogue continues.

I sent this text to his Western health practitioner.

Wife
Observation:
He is suffering in acute stage depression,
fear,
anxiety,
being incapable of decision making,
insomnia,
and suicidal thoughts.
I have not seen him in three months. He
is very involved in work out of state.
His response to depression is work addiction.
He is not responsive to me.

The allopathic physician wants to
place him on medication.
It is difficult to watch someone you have been
with for almost thirty-seven years have a Band-Aid
put on a symptom rather than finding root cause.

The doctor scheduled an appointment.

Wife's E-mail to Husband:
Her heart aches, and nausea goes to her gut.
She is in deep grief and sorrow about a
relationship she thought would not end
if both parties tried to show and
express love toward each other.
Neither can see that expression
of love from each other.
Then he took a job in another
state and just left her.
He said he loves her.
He faded out of the relationship slowly.
Then he just stopped coming home.
No holding.
No loving.
No kind words.
He just left.
She stayed away to sort things out.
Nausea and pain comes in waves.
Her dogs comfort her and kiss her
tears rolling down her cheeks.
The man she thought she knew for forty
years is gone without a trace of love or
friendship or kindness—no effort.
No white knight, no last-ditch effort.
He stays at work.
Her heart is broken.
She can't believe this.
Why?

Husband's
Silence.

Wife's Thoughts
She feels his fear resonating
from him in cyberspace.
There's clearly no trust.
Disbelief.
Positive thoughts change to negative.
After all these years,
WOW.
A human so paralyzed.

Therapist
Realization often comes with an unexpected
jolt that often makes us stronger.
Stay with truth.
This is no time for expectations.

Wife Texts Her Husband, Again
Because of his distancing over these months
(his choice), he avoids personal holidays.
She sees no closeness.
She no longer has an interest in having
him walk the dogs. She no longer has an
interest in cooking or cleaning for him.
She is capable of doing her own marketing.
Her needs, that he knows, is buying her olives!
She finds it difficult to watch him take
over space or withdraw completely.
She cannot be comfortable in his presence.
He cannot make amends at a social level.
She no longer has the energy to carry him.
He has taken thirty-plus days off from
work and has no interest in seeing her.
He mentions a visit Thanksgiving weekend.
She thinks of all the preparation
necessary for someone who will not be
present and who will return to work.
He does not show for a time to
help restore the relationship.
She did not want him to ruin a national
holiday memory with his suicidal thoughts.
Perhaps he should visit his brothers
and sister instead.

She no longer has the energy to carry him.
He wants to downsize to a small one-bedroom
apartment where he works out of state.
His choice makes it
clear he has no interest in having her there.
When there is no crisis, he says, "I," "I," "I."
Now in crisis, it is "we."
Before downsizing, she asks him to speak to his
boss, ask him for help, perhaps have his boss
pay for her to visit him if he is so exhausted,
renegotiate his contract.

Husband
Silence.
Then he says he is concerned about paying
out of his retirement account for taxes.
He says all the retirement money will be gone.
If this problem is not fixed, we will
have nothing to fall back on.

*(All of this not hearing and no response is odd.
Rational decisions are no longer coming from
the man I loved. All of this is coming from the
disease of clinical depression.)*

Text message dialogue continues:

Wife
Why did you cancel Ayurvedic treatment?
Concerned.
Calling the police to see if you are okay.
(Wife receives an annoyed phone call.)

Time passes.
Wife
Plane on time.

Wife
Landed.
Wearing polka-dot jacket.

Husband
Just got off freeway.

Wife
Okay.

Wife
My prayer to you each day is to be happy.
Each day be grateful.

Wife
Found my birthday present.

Husband
What store is this?
Where is it?
(She offers information. He does nothing.
He misses another of his wife's birthdays.)

Wife
I am on the plane. Looks like it's departing on time.

Husband
Glad we could have hot chocolate together.
Have a safe flight home.

Wife
Thank you for treating me to hot chocolate.
You were on the cell phone.
I had a hot chocolate. You had a hot chocolate.
My prayer to you each day is to be happy.
Each day be grateful.

Husband
I have landed in Chicago.
Are you home yet?

Wife
No, in air. Many delays.

Husband
Are you there yet?

Wife
Just landed.

Husband
Good. Glad you made it.

Wife
(now paying bills)
Need charge card clarification. What is FT?

Husband
Subscription to FT.
I called to reverse it.
I should know on Monday or Tuesday if it will be.

Wife
Why cancel?
You love that paper.

Husband
No response.

Wife
All I wanted from you was to hold
me and comfort me.
Did not realize it costs so much in your mind.

Husband
No response.

Wife
All I wanted from you was to hold me and comfort
me. Did not realize it costs so much in your mind.

Husband
No response.

Wife
All I wanted from you was to hold me
and comfort me, I did not realize it
costs so much in your mind.
(This seemed like such a simple concept to me.)
You can't even call regularly, not
that this is a substitute.
You actually used to call regularly. I
just can't understand any of this.
I don't know how someone dies inside
and can be so successful at work.

I guess you can't understand even
in my frustration I needed love and
understanding and holding from you.
*(The wife just did not understand this lack
of response was due to his illness. She took
this personally. She did not understand.)*

Husband
No response.

Wife
Resends.

Husband
No response.

Wife
Resends.

Husband
No response.

Wife
Resends and resends and resends.

Husband
No response.

Wife
I guess I am exhausted because I have
tried so hard for two people and failed.
You don't even tell me about work, what
the hotel was like, what you ate, who
you are hiring, why you are hiring?
This all leads to not knowing.

Husband
No response.

Wife
Really?
Forgot you have nothing to say to me anymore.
Really?
After thirty-six years?
You can't even respond?

Husband
No response.

Wife
By the way, this info is an offering
of help to get you back.
You don't respond. You don't want help.
Please don't rely on the feeling that no one
gives you answers, suggestions, and wisdom.
You don't want to hear, and you
ignore the ways to take action.

Husband
No response.

Wife
I guess this is it.
I get it.
Goodbye.
(She didn't get it. It was not that she was being ignored, or that there was a lack of love. This was his clinical depression.)

Wife
Just checking, are you calling at 2:00 p.m. my time or your time?

Wife
Surprised you did not call back as you said. Hope you are feeling better.

Husband
No response.

Husband
The car looks cool! Thank you for the picture. *(Referring to a car rental.)*

Wife
Please send me your current biweekly pay statement that includes deductions.

Wife
It is ironic you are so eager because
you had to wait nine months for this
new person to be hired at work.
That certainly trumps thirty-six years for me.
How little I am worth.

Husband
No response.

Wife
Did you receive my message about
pay statements? Please respond.
Let me know when you will send them.
Respond!

Husband
No response.

Wife
Respond so I can release this from my mind.

Wife
Thank you for your response.
(He finally sent statements.)

Husband
No response.

Wife
My sadness is you had to go elsewhere to work.
Much love, health, and joy.

Husband
No response.
*(This inability to respond was due to the
fatigue of clinical depression.)*

Wife
My dream was for us to share adventures and
sit at home appreciating each other and
reading comedies and sacred texts together.
I am saddened you have lost this
understanding of us and as in your
quote, "I am too much trouble."
My wishes are simply for your healing so you
may be happy and in your right mind. This is so
difficult for me because I am so deeply devoted
to you and you are so deeply devoted to work.

Wife
The Ayurvedic treatments you have
gifted me were of great help.
Thank you.
In the past you responded. I hope
you are being taken care of.
*(I thought he was involved with someone
else since he did not respond to me.
This was not true. His lack of responsiveness
was because of his clinical depression.)*

Husband
No response.

Then he responded.

Husband
I am glad the Ayurvedic treatments have been a great gift. I am not being taken care of. I am struggling to take care of myself. I know that you are devoted to my welfare and feel deeply for me. I have been meditating on all you have done for me over the years—the moves, the meals, the support for my work. I feel deeply that I have failed to understand and support you at the level you have needed. This saddens me greatly because this failure is my responsibility alone. I will love you forever. No one could ever take your place in my heart.

Wife
Nor you.
Love is included in devotion.
I am sorry your guilt is so deep that
you find me too difficult to deal with
because I want to be in your life.
It was not all bad. It is just that this past year the negatives greatly outweighed the positives, and there was no interest in discussion, compromise, or change. Am I too much trouble because I am a reminder of growing older?

Husband
No, you are not too much trouble. I am diverted from healthy activities by my concern about money and economic survival in a very hostile world.

Wife
This is a false concern from illness. One needs very little if one is at peace with one's self.

Wife
I am waiting for your call.

Husband
Will call around four thirty or five.
Just finishing errands.
Need to eat.
(He never called.)

Wife
There is only one person trying here.
Enough is enough.

Husband
I hope you get some rest today and recover from your trip.
Thinking of you. Sweet dreams.

Wife
Very sick chest.
Have to work today.

Husband
Did you catch a cold?

Wife
The Ayurvedic treatment released
deep sorrow and grief.

Husband July 2014
Dear wife,
I made it to my Ayurvedic treatment this
week. I had a private meeting with the doctor
today and discussed both my depression
and our relationship issues. I would like to
discuss this with you. I know you are still
recovering from your trip. What would be
a good time to call you tomorrow?
Love, Husband

Wife
*(He never made time for this discussion.
He went back to work.)*

Husband
I made it to the airport.

Husband
I made it to the connection.

Husband
I made it to the apartment.

Wife
Happy to hear you are safe.

Wife
Look—I know I am not a priority. Just call
or text every day from work to let me know
you are among the living. Thank you.
Please acknowledge you received
this message in a timely fashion.

Wife
Guess you still must be out enjoying
the long weekend.
Glad you are having fun.

Wife
Guess you really don't understand.

Husband
I am at the office safely.

Wife
Thank you.
The Memory Clinic called. Call back.

Husband
I am at the office safely.

Wife
Thank you.

Husband
I made it to the apartment safely.

Wife
Thank you.

Husband
Dearest wife, good morning. I am at the office safely.

Wife
Good morning. Thank you.

Husband
I made it back to the apartment safely. Have fun with your friends.

Wife
Really lovely women.

Husband
Good morning. I made it to the office safely.
I am glad that you had a good time last night.

Husband
I made it to the apartment safely.

Wife
Every day is not the same. These bits
should be shared in a relationship.

Husband
I slept in.
Checking into bathtubs now.
*(She requested him to check on
tubs for a new apartment.)*

Wife
Thank you.
I actually think you like feeling sorry for yourself
more than you like me or anyone else.

Husband
Good morning. I do not feel sorry for myself.
I feel trapped by my bad decisions and am
trying to come to terms with them every day.
I made it to the office safely.

Husband
I worked late and am safely at the apartment.
(These short answers were trying to comply with my requests of communication. With his clinical depression, this was the best he could do.)

Husband
Good morning. I made it safely to the office for early calls to Europe.

Husband
I worked late and made it back
to the apartment safely.

Wife
I am really disappointed with you.
It amazes me that you are so insensitive.
If your routine changes, advance notice
is nice so I am prepared for you coming
home later, especially when I have to go
to bed early for my early day at work.
Is this your anger? Is this just you hating me?
I feel like a mother or a teacher, something
you force me to be because of your lack
of love and compassion toward me.
I deserve at least this consideration. You
can put me in your calendar, yet you
continually express this bad behavior.

This is exactly what brings on my anger.
One week you can be kind, and
the next week you disappear.
I cannot bear this roller coaster of insensitivity
and lack of compassion and love.

Husband
I am sorry. I was working on preparing for
the BOD meeting and worked late to do
so. I forgot that this was your early night
because of class tomorrow morning. I want
to come see you at the end of next week.
Am I welcome to come?

Wife
Our nieces are in town, and I am busy
on Wednesday and Thursday.
Planning in advance is useful.
Perhaps another time on neutral ground.
*(This happened to be his birthday. The last
two years he did not acknowledge our
anniversary or my last two years of birthdays.)*

Husband
I am working in the apartment this morning.

Husband
I made it to the office safely.

Husband
I am going to a BOD meeting now at a downtown restaurant. I will let you know when I arrive at the apartment this evening.

Wife
Thank you.

Husband
I am safely at the apartment. Dinner at a cafe downtown. I had kale Caesar salad, halibut with vegetables, and a variant of strawberry shortcake. Sweet dreams.

Husband
I am safely at the BOD meeting on the seventy-fifth floor of a downtown office building.
(I thought why did he mentioned seventy-fifth floor? What is he thinking? OMG should I be concerned?)

Husband
I made it back to the apartment safely.
(I think, what a relief. He is safe.)

Husband
I made it to the BOD meeting safely.

Husband
I am at the apartment, exhausted after
the BOD meeting. I will call tomorrow.

Husband
I have been making calls to Europe
this morning at the apartment and
am going to the office now.

Husband
I made it to the office safely.

Husband
I made it back to the apartment safely. I
am making dinner and going to bed early.
I hope you and the dogs are safe.

Husband
I made it to the office safely.

Husband
I made it to the apartment safely. I know you have
an early day tomorrow. I hope you sleep well.

Husband
I am working at the apartment.

Wife
Congrats on another year!
BTW, good wishes from your sister-in-law. "Tell him happy birthday!" Did you just stay at your apartment today?

Wife
Thanks for your immediate response.

Husband
I stayed in to rest. How is your client?

Wife
Badly injured, with lots of fractures and swelling. It's funny, but in spite of all the pain, he said this was the best thing that ever happened to him because it brought his family closer together with a more serious understanding of mortality.

Husband
I hope he recovers without further complications. I am concerned about his flying after his collapsed lung.
(When it came to work modalities, he was able to briefly come out of his presentation of depression.)

Wife
He is thinking of flying.

Husband
I would think this trip is dangerous.
I am at my office working today.
Have a great day.

Wife
Got some of his swelling down in his ankles.
Ayurvedic massage training is amazing.

Husband
Just got back and had a late dinner. I am
glad that you are able to help with your skills.
I have an early call tomorrow morning.

Husband
I had my early call and made
it to the office safely.

Husband
I made it back to the apartment
for an early dinner. I have to review
the submission later tonight.

Husband
I made it to the office safely. I'm still
working on the submission.

Wife
Wishing you success.

Husband
I made it back to the apartment safely.

Husband
I made it back to the office safely.

Husband
I made it to the apartment safely.

Husband
I made it to my office safely.

Husband
I made it back to the apartment safely. I was excited by your idea when you called. I am sorry you changed your mind about the trip.

Wife
I did not change my mind. You were ambivalent, and I needed a definite answer, not, "That sounds interesting."
Stop the games.
(This was my expression of frustration toward my husband who presented with this illness.)

Husband
I am resting at the apartment.

Wife

I just couldn't live in sadness, though I am sad sometimes, at which point I have to pull myself somewhere to be with people or take the dogs on a walk or check out wildlife.
It saddens me you don't have an interest to wake up next to someone to say, "Good morning, I love you."
It sickens me that for so long I had a false hope of enjoying this sort of relationship with you and tried so hard to have this. I thought you wanted this too, and I inflicted these needs on someone who has no interest in this.
It is difficult for me yet necessary to move away from this husband, the beloved physician, because every day there is a pang of sadness, knowing I am not wanted.
This is my reality check. Don't say, "I want this too," because you don't make this happen. My reality check is that I am very alone and sad because I am alone.
(I was asking for the impossible due to his illness, and I just didn't know this.)

Husband

I know that I have not been able to give you the kind of attention and love that you need. I think back at evenings of television instead of talking and card games. too much travel for business, and too little travel for pleasure with you, too much concern for what my work colleagues think of me and too little concern for your happiness, too much concern for the outward trappings of what money can buy and too little thought for long-term stability. I think about these mistakes every day and can see no way out of their consequences. I live from day to day as best as I can. I have allowed my mania for professional stature to overwhelm my need for personal happiness with a caring person who was always concerned with my well-being.

Wife
Thank you for acknowledging
you have made a choice.
You have chosen work.
I've got it.
It's hard to sink in even if I already knew.
I promise it will.
(This was my response of sadness and frustration and anger to him for succumbing to his illness.)

Husband
I am not making a choice for work. I feel trapped in work with no way out that I can see. I miss you and the life I had with you when we lived together in the same state. That is why I wanted to visit you.

Wife
*(Visit me? We should be living together. I am
your wife. I thought this, I did not text this.)*
I will try not to bother you with any
more questions or comments.
Thank you for your continued financial support,
since long ago I gave up a real income
job for you and your dreams.

Husband
I realize that you gave up a real income
job for me and my dreams. These dreams
have turned into a nightmare for me. I want
to hear your questions and comments.
Please do not stop sending them.

Wife
I'm finished.
A lawyer will contact you.
*(I had hoped this would shock him into
returning to health—my ignorance.)*

Husband
What do you mean about a lawyer?

Wife
If you were so alone, you would have invited me
to your place for special weekends. Stop the BS.

Husband
I made it to the office safely. Did you get what
you needed for the insurance question?
Can you come here for the
weekend of August 16?

Wife
Possibly. What is happening?
(I feared that he would let me down again.)

Husband
I am back in the apartment
safely. There is no event.
(August 27 is our anniversary.)
I was hoping to spend time with
you exploring this area.

Wife
What about the dogs?
Will you be staring at the cell phone
all the time like the last visit?
Will there be time to settle things?
Will you answer historic questions
without prompting?

Husband
I have not decided where to explore yet.
I will not be working or looking at the cell.
I have not thought about details yet. We
will have time to talk about things

Wife
Hmmm.
Would this incomplete offering
be acceptable at work?

Husband
Just consider it.

Wife
It?

Husband
The trip.
*(I would fly into his arms if I knew he
would be mentally present.)*

Husband
I have been in meetings all afternoon.
I will call you around 5:00 p.m.

Wife
Not necessary.
(I was working.)

Husband
I called but could not reach you.
I will try again tomorrow.
(He did not call.)

Husband
I am at the office in a meeting. I will call
you back as soon as I am finished.

Husband
I am at the apartment safely.

Husband
I am at the office. I have settled the bill for the
MRI so you do not have to be concerned about it.

Husband
I am at the apartment. I stayed in resting today.

Husband
I am at the apartment resting. I have a
trip to Boston tomorrow and Tuesday.

Wife
Have fun.

Husband
I made it to the airport safely. We started
meetings at ten and finished at six. It
will be a long but interesting day.

Husband
I am taking off now.

Husband
I am at the hotel safely.

Wife
Nice.

Husband
I am at the hotel. I'm going to the meeting soon.

Wife
Do you remember name of mortgage company? A friend reeds info.

Husband
Name given.

Wife
Thank you.

Husband
I am at the office safely.

Husband
I am at the apartment safely.

Husband
I am working at the apartment today. I am spending the rest of the day at the apartment. I hope you are well.
(There was no further mention of the invitation to visit him.)

Husband
I made it to the office safely.

Husband
I made it to the apartment safely.

Husband
I am at the office working.

Husband
I am back at the apartment.

Wife
Not me.

Husband
Where are you?

Wife
Philosophically or physically—
ahh, that is the question.

Wife
Question: What do you intend to do
with these realizations you have been
having through your meditations?

Husband
Answer: I intend to change my behavior
toward you, my family, and others.

Wife
When?
How?
In what order?

Who are the others?
Hope you are feeling better.
Are you taking herbs for your cold?
They are okay to take with other herbs.
Are you at work?
Break the routine.

Wife
Please use this prayer:
"May my heart be filled with
love and compassion.
May my mind be filled with
understanding and peace.
May my hands be filled with selfless service.
May my home be filled with
abundance and harmony.
May my life be filled with health and prosperity.
May my inner being be filled with wisdom.
-Peace, prosperity and joy to
all." (Brahma Kumaris).

Wife
How did your session go with the accountant?

Husband
It went well. I am continuing to be worried about money for good reason. Although we have paid each quarter as the accountant said, I could not pay the full amount that I should have, so we are behind for the year. Therefore, we will have to take money out of the retirement account

again and then have to pay tax on it in 2014.
It is very depressing to see the money we worked
so hard for go to the government in taxes, all
because of a single mistake we made in 2011 of
not holding on to the cash. *(This was a reference
to buying our house outright, a positive effort.)* I am
sharing this with you so you have the details you
need to understand what is going on. This was
the theme of our session: giving you more
information so you feel included and valued.

Wife
Get off the house.
You told me to sell the apartment,
which was paid for.
The house is mine. You gave it to me as
a replacement for the apartment.
Stop trying to make me feel
bad about your mistake.
This is what comes of no discussion.
*(This house was given to me for safekeeping,
for our retirement, since he was not thinking
rationally and could create more debt.)*

Wife
Your money concerns are not with good reason.
The house is not a mistake.
Are you staying at work for the holidays,
including Thanksgiving? You say you cannot
handle anger, yet you prick a wound until
you make it bleed again and again.

Husband
You still do not see the situation
by the WMD of 2013.

Wife
I do not understand the initials again,
my friend. Full disclosure.
*(Text messages were his only
communication toward the end.
He stopped calling.)*

A friend paraphrased a comment by Dick
Cavett, who also suffered from depression, that
if someone had an instant cure for cancer,
the patient would travel to the far ends of the
earth; for someone who is clinically depressed,
if there were a magic pill to cure depression
just across the room, the sufferer would not
have the energy to get up and take the pill.

He did not call me this weekend. He did not text
me this weekend. I thought I would just let him
rest. I would wait until he felt like calling me.

I received a call from his boss Monday
morning at seven forty-five.
He committed suicide. He hung himself at work.

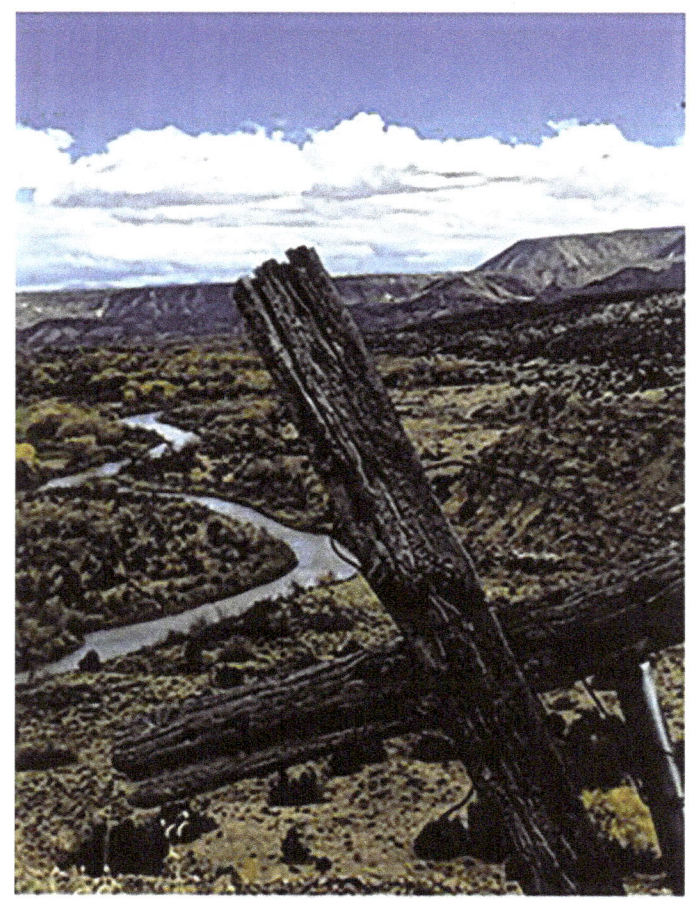

Excerpts from the Autopsy

The coronary arteries show atherosclerosis with approximately 85 percent stenosis of the proximal right coronary artery and no significant stenosis in all other major coronary arteries. The left ventricle is mildly dilated. The distal aorta shows prominent calcific atherosclerosis with plaque.

This sixty-seven-year-old man who was found deceased in the stairwell of a parking garage died of asphyxia due to hanging. Based on the findings of the investigation and autopsy, the manner of death is certified as suicide.

Trying To Understand This Illness

My husband and I had an injured relationship for many years. The root cause of depression was never really addressed. He was a brilliant man living inside his mind.

He worked endlessly on the challenges and discoveries and joys of work. He laughed and shared and allowed his goodness and ego to spill over onto others, and he was happy at work.

The appearance of happiness at work was a performance that consumed all of his energy. This took a great deal of effort for a man who lived inside his head.

When he came home, he shared his exhaustion
with me. He stared into space and television.
He couldn't hear me. He didn't even eat
a well-prepared meal at the dining room
table. He sat in front of the television, gulping
down food in silence. There was nothing left
of him to build and develop and maintain
a relationship of sharing and feeling with
another human being at an equal level.

For some reason, I accepted this because
he said his work was for both of us. I was sad
and ached over this. I thought I had never
taken the right action to bring the joy and
laughter and communication with him.

I thought he should communicate at home
because he did at work. He finally told me
this person at home was who he really was.
At work, he was just doing good acting.

The pain made me question why I stayed. It was because of our marriage vows—"till death do us part."

In understanding his death, we need to understand progression of disease.

It begins with stress. If he had only taken time out for a few deep breaths when he was anxious or sad. He ignored this.

Just do one more thing. Disease escalates into clinical depression.

Events and lifestyle (demands at work and overworking to please, to be accepted, and to get that pat by his boss) make this disease flourish.

He couldn't make it stop. I, who did not suffer, said, "Get over it. Be happy." I did not understand that this was like asking a diabetic to stop taking insulin and be healthy.

This black hole he was in was like stage IV cancer. The demons of pain and suffering wipe out happiness and joy. The sufferer learns to isolate himself to be able to end his pain and suffering through suicide.

I must forgive myself.
I must share.
I must talk about mental illness.
I must listen with love and compassion,
so we all can hear,
so we all can heal.

I couldn't stop it.
I watched.
I begged.
I suggested.
I got angry.
I demanded.
I sought support.
I couldn't stop it.
I watched the downward spiral.
I was helpless.
I felt a sinking pit in my stomach.
I was a witness.
Suicide is not a peaceful death.
It is violent, and people left
behind see the violence and
after effects on others.

For me, there seems to be so much more.
For him, he had enough.

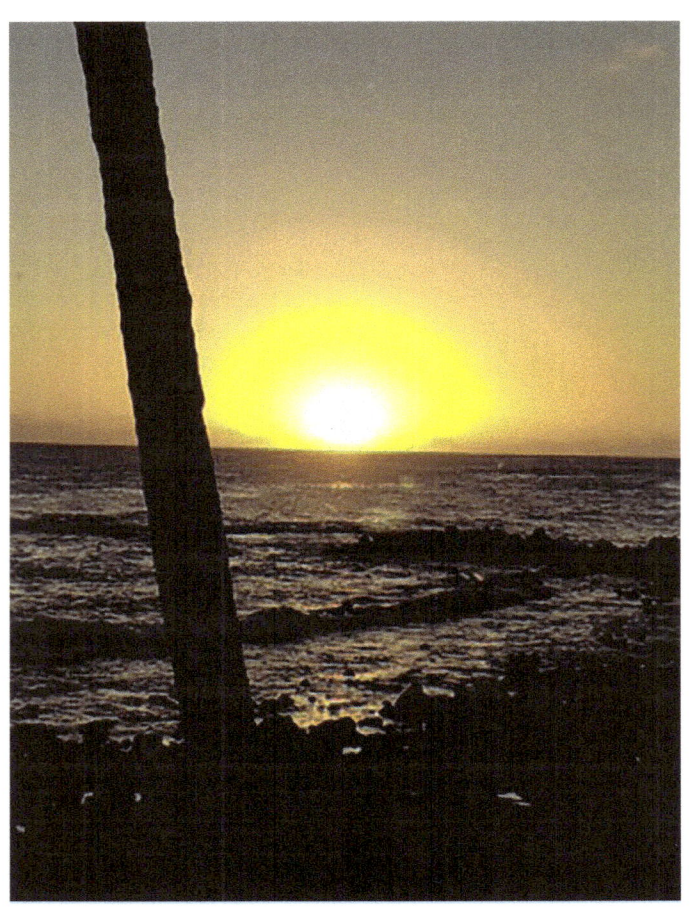

Sometimes writing thoughts down prevent them from eating away at you. Depression seems to sever the relctionship of heart and mind. Mind overwhelms the heart.

The memory of his depression and suicide is an annoying hum. With time, the hum is reduced.

Eastern and Western Medical Explanations for Clinical Depression

Eastern medicine (Ayurveda) describes disease progression through six stages. The progression of depression is as follows:

- The first stage is accumulation of depression, where negative thoughts or sad thoughts begin.
- The second stage is provocation, causing aggravation of a site where the negative thoughts get stuck in sadness, creating fatigue, withdrawal, and lies to avoid reality.
- The third stage is spread, where changes move to other tissues. Here the mind consumes or overwhelms the heart.
- The fourth stage is qualitative change, where the aggravation moves to a weakened site, being the heart; the heart closes, and blockage occurs.
- The fifth stage is manifestation, where symptoms of disease can be observed. This is when heart vessels block, especially seen with the blockage of coronary arteries.
- The sixth stage is differentiation, where the disease leads to destruction and alteration of tissue. Here the heart breaks.

The heart cttacks itself (heart attack) or suicide.² In Western medicine, studies also express clinical depression as a risk factor for coronary artery disease in men, demonstrating clinical depression is an independent risk factor for incident coronary artery disease.³

---

² Vasant Lad, MASC, *Textbook of Ayurveda: A Complete Guide to Clinical Assessment*, Volume 2, chapter 2 (Albuquerque, NM: The Ayurvedic Press, 2006).
³ Daniel E. Ford, MD, MPH, et al. "Original Investigation, Depression Is a Risk Factor for Coronary Artery Disease in Men, the Precursors Study," *Arch Intern Med*, Vol. 158, July 13, 1998, 1422, American Medical Association.

Through Ayurveda I also discovered that the
discussion of depression is incomplete without
discussing the five elements we are made of:
gas or space,
air,
fire,
water,
and *earth.*
Each of us are differently weighted or
balanced with more or less of some
of these elements than others.
These elements present variations on depression.
Usually the primary elements are the first to
indicate the imbalance of depression.
When secondary and tertiary elements
become involved, the fifth and sixth
stages of disease play out through clinical
depression—suicide or heart failure.

Air and Space Depression
too much space creating:
isolation
fear
self-doubt
insecurity
with no delinection
pushing and crushing the individual's true nature

•

Fire and Water Depression
Too much heat and movement creating:
Self-centering
arrogance
work addiction
piercing, pushing and crushing the self

•

Earth and Water Depression
Weighing down the individual
greed
heaviness
being stuck
congestion
pushing depression into the heart
causing congestive heart failure.

He was made up of the five
elements with this variation:
His primary elements were *fire and water*.
His secondary elements were *earth and water*.
His tertiary elements were *air and space*.

From grade school, he could be described
with depression and balance at his
primary level of fire and water.
In balance, he was educated,
analytical, and brilliant.
Out of balance, he showed tendencies toward
arrogance, study addiction, judgment, and
piercing comments and observations.

His last fourteen years expressed his
secondary elements of earth and water.
In balance, he could be described as
methodical, patient, and steady.
Out of balance, he showed tendencies
of greed, heaviness, being stuck, and
congestion (especially in the heart).

The year before his death by suicide, he did suffer from right coronary artery blockage that was undetected until the autopsy.

His third set of qualities were of air and space. In balance, he could be described as having expansive thought and creativity. Out of balance, he was isolated, fearful, and filled with insecurity and self- doubt, with no delineation in judgment.

He was able to maintain this balanced side at work but not at home or in his emotional life.

"His illness came from an overly powerful mind. In such an individual, there is over confidence and suppression of emotions and physical symptoms. Even though the person may have severe pain, he does not show it. This person is in denial and this can mislead a doctor and prevent treatment."[4]

"When healthy, the fire element brings joy, happiness, contentment and cheerfulness. When a person laughs his fire element is healthy. When the fire element is abnormal, there is unhappiness, grief, sadness and depression. Fire governs secretion of neurotransmitters and neuro-chemical synthesis of sensation and perception, which becomes understanding. This understanding is higher Cerebral activity and comes from the healthy fire element. If this digestive fire is low this can become chemical depression."[5]

---

[4] Vasant Lad, MASC, *Textbook of Ayurveda: Principles of Management and Treatment*, Volume 3 (Albuquerque, NM: The Ayurvedic Press, 2012).

[5] Vasant Lad, MASC, *Textbook of Ayurveda: Fundamental Principles of Ayurveda*, Volume 1 (Albuquerque, NM: The Ayurvedic Press, 2002), 87.

At some level, we are the cause of our own suffering, be it genetics, illness, or personal choice.

The disease progresses through diet,
lifestyle, behavior, and genetics.

Improving Communication

Can we listen to the whole story of depression?

Observe?

Self-explore?

Witness?

Listen.
Bear witness.

Many times we hear things that shock us.
It prevents us from asking questions that
may help us understand. Sometimes when
we hear someone who is depressed or is
doing something in a different way than
we would do, we block information.

We stop the conversation because we don't know
how to continue the conversation. Sometimes
information is difficult to digest, and here we lose
the dialogue with depression. We don't have the
right questions. We don't have open ears to listen.
Clinically depressed people are ill. They are not
healthy, so they are different. We are all different
from each other. This creates difficulty in hearing
because we talk instead of bearing witness.

It takes time to hear information we do not
understand or that is incompatible to our own
thoughts. This new information takes time to
digest and accept. When we do, we discover
that both sides have truth and wisdom. We
develop compassion and understanding.
We must learn to validate others by hearing.
We must validate ourselves by hearing.

Truth is truth.

An Outsider's Thoughts on Depression

We can study them. We can advise
them. We can block them.
We *cannot* remove the dark hole.
Do they have the tools to get
themselves out of the dark hole?
Where can they find the tools
to rise above or dig out?
We need to get the sufferers of depression to
tell us what would be useful, but they do not
know themselves and are usually paralyzed
mentally from the disease of clinical depression.
How can we help them get out of the
dark hole or remove the black cloud?
We should not feel superior.
We don't understand this disease and the pain.
We can only see the surface of their illness.
We do not know depression's depths. If we did,
could we prevent the end stage of depression?
Depression comes from different sources.
There are many different types.
We must recognize this.
It is like discussing cancer. There are so
many different kinds of cancer, some
curable, some that can go into remission,
while other cancers are incurable.

We must talk with those that suffer.
We must hear the sufferer.
We must not take this personally but objectively.
We cannot fix this disease.

We need their help.
We need them to talk.
We need to listen.

Only they can heal with proper tools:

Exercise
Diet
Lifestyle
Change
Therapy
Herbs and medicines
They must have neutral ground
to express their feelings.
We must try to understand.

Depression is at epidemic proportions. One in four American adults suffer from mental illness. That is approximately 61.5 million people.[6]

According to National Alliance on Mental Health, 260 million antidepressant prescriptions are filled each year. The total population in the United States is 321 million.

With little long-term research, scientists explore new methods to tell when patients are ready to go off medication. Reasons for continuing medication reduces the risk of relapse of depression by about 50 percent. With each relapse, the risk of an additional bout of depression increases by 16 percent. Reasons for stopping antidepressant medication is their side effects, like weight gain and sexual dysfunction. Women may want to stop before getting pregnant or nursing.

More than 303 million prescriptions were filled for antidepressants and mood-stabilizing drugs in 2014, according to IMS Health, which tracks pharmaceutical sales.[7]

---

[6] *AARP, the Magazine*, September 2015, volume 58, #5b, 48.
[7] *The Wall Street Journal*, Tuesday, March 8, 2016, d1.

More statistics:

As of 2017, 300 million people around the world have depression according to The World Health Association.

According to Data from a 2017 National survey on Drug use and Health, 17.3 million adults in the United States- equaling 7.1% of all adults in the country- have experienced a major depressive episode in the past year according to the National Institute of Mental Health(NIH) This is pre COVID!

Depression is the leading cause of disability world wide, quoted from very.wellmind.com

Programs for Depression Assistance:

Confidential 24 hour a day support
Samaritans 24 hour Crisis hotline
212-673-3000

United Way Helpline
1-800-233-4357

National Alliance on Mental Illness (NAMI)

National Institute of Mental Health (NIH)

Substance Abuse and Mental Health Services Administration (SAMHSA)National helpline
1-800-662-4357

Falling down is part of life.
Getting back up is living.
—Anonymous[8]

---

[8] QuotableTM Cards, 263.

The Questions for the Living

How will I get through this event?
How will I continue with my life?
What happens next?
I am older.
My financial situation has radically changed.
My husband was the high-income earner.
I earned monies, that he considered
as a write-off for taxes.
I went through tears.
I was frustrated.
I was angry.
I had to move on.
I tried to center myself so I could
move, so I could work, so I could.

My grounding has to happen every
day so I can maintain my stability.
My daily routine is thanking the planet
for allowing me to be present. I need to
focus on breathing so I can take full, deep
breaths to help calm and center myself.
Then I must focus on movement to maintain
physical strength, flexibility, and endurance.
Movement can be walking,
cycling, stretching, or yoga.
The next focus is on positive affirmations.
Then it is important to keep in touch with
friends because sometimes they are
concerned about contacting you, since
they too are disturbed by this end.
Friends may not know how to approach the
one left behind because they do not want to
cause more pain or appear insensitive. Find
support groups; people who have suffered similar
events teach you how to witness and listen.
Get something done each day.
Focus on the positive.
The bad thoughts and bad feelings
will soften over time.
Everything takes time.

Facts, Not Fiction

Depression is treated through psychiatry,
medicine, psychology, and talk
therapy in the United States.

Some medicines are created to block depression
and numb feelings that become trapped in the
mind, putting pressure on the heart until it breaks
physically or by suicide, which ends the dialogue.

Suppressing thoughts through medicine is a way
one may continue to function in life or in work.

The blocking of the disease never allows the
person who suffers from the illness to get to the
root cause of the illness to help understand
him or herself and undo the weaving of
many years or generations of suffering.

The medication allows the person
to function at base level.
Epidemic proportions of drugs are being used,
shifting society from truth and compassion
to shallowness, numbness, and death.

Therapy is also used. The challenge for the
therapist is to translate healthy action to someone
who suffers from the demons of depression.

For the clinically depressed person,
being happy is a foreign language.
Movement through exercise is impossible due
to the weight of disease the patient bears.
Breathing fully is difficult because the sufferer
feels he is in a dark hole, an enclosed space.
Discussion can begin to resolve the mental
pain. Unfortunately, this therapy often does
not continue to take the individual beyond the
threshold of the dark hole, and the patient falls
back in. With understanding of the individual's
issues, there is this momentary exit from the hole.
Then with realization and awareness of how
this disease has affected his or her loved
ones, the sufferer falls back into the dark
hole where no one can reach him or her.
The therapist is not capable of jumping in
with proper tools to bring them both out.

At this point, the earth closes in, and the person
is buried in isolation with suicidal thoughts, using
his or her tools to develop suicide into reality.

That is the end game of depression.

Held by the Universe

There is a key factor to joy and happiness. I
think I am beginning to recognize this key.
It is not your fault.
You cannot fix things for other people.
You are okay.
Be kind to yourself. It is not your fault.
You cannot fix others from the outside.
You are a good person ...
I am a good person.
It is not my fault.
We may see things in others that seem to
be simple fixes. We must let this go.
Everyone is on their own path.
We are on our own paths of
forgiveness, of love, of life.
*I am on my own path. I am a good
person. I am not to blame.*
It is not my fault.
I cannot fix someone else.
*I cannot take care of someone else who
does not want to be taken care of.*
*I must do unto myself as I do
kindnesses unto others.*
I am a good person.
It is not my fault.
I am not alone. We are not alone.
When we feel we are alone, we are not
connected to the universe. The awareness and
healing come from knowing we are part of the
universe. We hold the universe and it holds us.

And This Is Not the End

Here I am becoming a person with
new responses, new reactions that
help me learn and grow.

I am removing myself from the past, from my
husband's ego and fears, and his exaggerated
thoughts due to clinical depression.
I am learning the art of understanding so I can
lower the volume of turmoil from the past. I can
move on with my life and live in the present.
It is important to find new relationships
with their fresh beginnings and
endings and still remain whole.

We have been brought up with fairy tales with romance and happy endings. It is difficult to place these fairy tales into reality. But I do still believe in happily ever living and happily ever after with lessons learned, with no regrets. It helps to love life in the moment with compassion and caring, even for *me* this time around.
I seek kindness, enjoying love and laughter with friends. The heart can open again or close, and we have to choose a path.
This is my journey—clearing out past chaos, living with it, embracing it, and letting it go.

Here goes my giant step now…

It is a happy beginning.
It is time to reach out.

Life is catch and release, letting go, and receiving.

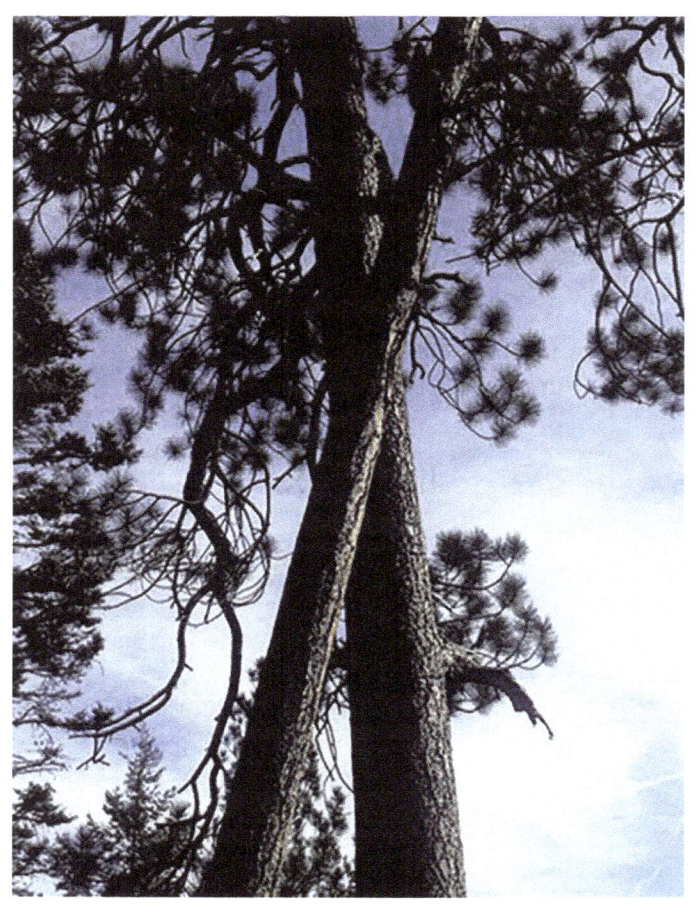

With thanks and gratitude I raise my glass
to many friends who have read and
re-read my manuscript. To my precious
editors who encouraged me to proceed,
bringing loose thoughts, punctuation,
pronouns and tenses together. Sharing
tears, solace, comfort and hope.

Pamela Schuyler

The author has chosen to center the text, as we should be centered in our lives to stay healthy and balanced.

Currently this author shares her books with her readers. She teaches yoga for the health of body, mind, and spirit.

www.ingramcontent.com/pod-product-compliance
Lightning Source LLC
Chambersburg PA
CBHW061728070526
44583CB00024B/3053